Inspirational Islamic Wisdom

With wisdom

from the Quran

of Muhammad

of Rumi

and of the four great caliphs

Legal notice

Bibliographic Information of the German National Library:
The German National Library lists this publication in the German National Bibliography;
detailed bibliographic data are available on the Internet at http://dnb.dnb.de.

© 2022 Pinar Akdag

Book cover: Canva.com

Translator: Henry Whittlesey

Printed and Published: BoD – Books on Demand, Norderstedt

ISBN: 978-3-7557-1252-7

...For a little more peace,
a little more understanding
between cultures
and for a little more
freedom, equality
and brotherhood
on earth.

Sincerely,
Pinar Akdag

Table of Contents

1. Spiritual Wisdom from the Quran

The Quran

- is the Holy Scripture of Islam;
- was first revealed near Mecca on Mount al-Nour in the month of Ramadan around 610 AD;
- was recited to Prophet Muhammad (s.a.w.) over a period of about 23 years;
- consists of 114 suras (sections), which are in turn comprised of ayet (verses).

Bismillahirrahmanirrahim (In the name of Allah, the Lord of Mercy, the Giver of Mercy)

1/1)
In the name of Allah, the Lord of Mercy, the Giver of Mercy!
1/2)
Praise be to Allah, Lord of all Worlds
1/3)
The Lord of Mercy, the Giver of Mercy
1/4)
Master of the Day of Judgement!
1/5)
It is You we serve; it is You we ask for help.
1/6)
Guide us to the right path,
1/7)
The path of those You have blessed, not those who incur your anger and not those who have gone astray.

2/29)
It was He (Allah) who created all that is on the earth for you ...

2/62)
The [Muslim] believers, the Jews, the Christians, and the Sabians – all those who believe in Allah and the Last Day and do good – will have their rewards with their Lord. No fear for them, nor will they grieve.

2/107)
Do you not know that control of the heavens and the earth belongs to Allah and Your [believers] have no protector or helper but Allah?

2/115)
The East and the West belong to Allah: Wherever you turn, there is Allah's Face. Allah is all-pervading and all-knowing.

2/118)
Those who have no knowledge also say, "If only Allah would speak to us!" or "If only a miraculous sign would come to us!" People before them said the same things: their hearts are all alike. We have made Our signs clear (enough) to people who have faith.

2/143)
We have made you [believers] into a community of the middle*, so that you are witnesses for the people.
*As a religion of the middle way, Islam is averse to anything extreme.

2/152)
So remember Me (Allah); I will remember you. Be thankful to Me, and never ungrateful.

2/153)
You who believe, seek help through steadfastness and prayer, for Allah is with the steadfast.

2/186)
And if My (Allah's) servants ask you about Me, I am near. I respond to those who call Me, so let them respond to Me and believe in Me, so that they may be rightly guided.

2/251)
... If Allah did not drive some back some people by means of others, the earth would be completely corrupt, but Allah is bountiful to all.

2/256)

There is no compulsion in religion...!*

*(This is both the prohibition against using force in matters of faith and a statement that such coercion would be an ineffectual attempt.)

2/279)

... You will not suffer loss or cause others to suffer loss.

2/281)

And beware of a Day when you will be returned to Allah. Every soul will be paid in full for what it has earned, and no one will be wronged.

3/7)

It is He who has sent the Scripture down to you (Muhammad). Some of its verses are unambiguous and clear – these are the cornerstones of the Scripture;* the others are ambiguous. The perverse at heart eagerly pursue the ambiguities in their attempt to make trouble and to pin down a specific meaning (of their own). Only Allah knows the true meaning. Those firmly grounded in knowledge say: "We believe in it. It is all from our Lord." Only those with real perception will take heed.

*the original text with God

3/108)

These are Allah's revelations. We recite them to you with the Truth. And Allah does not will injustice for His creatures, wherever they are in the world.

3/133)

Hurry towards your Lord's (Allah's) forgiveness and a Garden as wide as the heavens and earth prepared for the righteous,

3/134)

Who give, both in prosperity and adversity, who restrain their anger and pardon people – Allah loves those who do good.
3/135)
Those who remember Allah and implore forgiveness for their sins if they do something shameful or wrong themselves – who forgives sins but Allah? – and who never knowingly persist in doing wrong:
3/136)
The reward for such people is forgiveness from their Lord, and Gardens graced with flowing streams, where they will remain. How excellent is the reward of those who labor.

4/40)
Allah does not wrong anyone by as much as the weight of a speck of dust. He doubles any good deed and gives a tremendous reward of His own.

6/38)
All living beings roaming the earth and winged birds soaring in the sky are communities* like yourselves.
*or: "Creatures"

6/59)
He has the keys to the unseen; no one knows them but Him. He knows all that is in the land and sea. No leaf falls without His knowledge. Nor is there a single grain in the darkness of the earth, or anything, fresh or withered, that is not written in a clear Record.

6/60)
It is He who calls you back by night,* knowing what you have done by day, then raises you up again in the daytime until your fixed term is fulfilled. It is to Him that you will return in the end. And He will tell you what you have done.
*Souls return to God when you are asleep

6/102)
This is Allah, your Lord! There is no God but Him, the Creator of all things. So worship Him alone. He is in charge of all things.

6/103)
No vision can take Him in. But He takes in all vision. He is the All Subtle,* All Aware.
*Arabic: al-latif; can also mean the sensitive, kind, or gentle one.

6/132)
Everyone is assigned a rank according to their deeds. Your Lord is aware of anything they do.

6/145)
Say: "In all that has been revealed to me (Muhammad), I find nothing forbidden for people to eat, except for carrion, flowing blood, pig's meat – it is loathsome – or a sinful offering over which any name other than Allah's has been invoked."

6/160)
Whoever has done a good deed will have it ten times to their credit. But whoever has done a bad deed will be repaid only with its equivalent. They will not be wronged.

12/21)
... As Allah always prevails in His purpose, though most people do not realize it.

13/2)
It is Allah who raised up the heavens with no visible supports. Then He set Himself on the throne. And He has subjected the sun and the moon to his service. Each pursues its course for an appointed time. He regulates everything. He makes the signs clear so that you may be certain of meeting your Lord.

13/11)
Each person has angels before them and behind, watching over them in turns by Allah's command. Allah does not change the condition of people unless they change in themselves.

16/97)
To whoever, male or female, does good deeds and has faith, We shall give a good life. We shall reward them according to the best of their actions.

17/84)
Say: "Everyone does things their own way. But your Lord (Allah) is fully aware of who follows the right path."

20/113)
We have sent the Quran down in the Arabic tongue and given all kinds of warnings in it, so that they would be pious or He (Allah) would cause them to remember God.

20/135)
Say: "We are all waiting, So you carry on waiting. You will come to learn who has followed the straight and even path, and been rightly guided."

21/30)
Are the disbelievers not aware that the heavens and the earth used to be joined together* and that We ripped them apart,** that We made every living thing from water?*** Will they not believe?
* Highest-density hydrogen according to what we know today.
** In the so-called big bang
*** This, too, has been corroborated by history.

21/31)

And We put firm mountains on the earth, lest it should sway under them. And we set broad paths on it, so that they might follow the right direction.

21/32)

And We made the sky a well-secured canopy. Yet from His signs they turn away.

21/33)

It is He (Allah) who created night and day, the sun and the moon, each floating in its orbit.

21/34)

We have not granted everlasting life to any other human being before you either. So if you die, will they live forever?

21/35)

Every soul is certain to taste death. We test you all through the bad and the good. And to Us you will all return.

21/37)

Man was created hasty. I (Allah) will show you My signs soon, so do not ask Me to hasten them.

21/47)

We will set up scales of justice for the Day of Resurrection so that no one can be wronged in the least. And if there should be even the weight of a mustard seed, We shall bring it out. And we take excellent account.

24/35)

Allah is the Light of the heavens and earth. His Light is like this: There is a niche, and in it a lamp. The lamp inside a glass. And the glass is like a glittering star. It is fueled from a blessed tree, an olive tree, from neither east nor west, whose oil almost gives light even when no fire touches it. Light upon Light! Allah guides whoever He will to His Light. And Allah draws such comparisons for people. And Allah is knowing of all things.*

*The so-called verse of light, of particular importance in Islamic mysticism.

31/27)
If all the trees on earth were pens and all the seas (ink), with seven more seas besides, were filled: Still Allah's words would not run out! Allah is powerful and wise.

35/1)
Praise be to Allah, Creator of the heavens and earth, who made angels messengers with two, three, four [pairs of] wings. He adds to creation as He will. Allah has power over everything.

36/12)
We shall certainly bring the dead back to life. And We record what they have done as well as what they left behind. We keep an account of everything in a clear Record.

36/40)
The sun cannot overtake the moon, nor can the night outrun the day: each floats in its own orbit.

39/44)
Say: "All intercession belongs to Allah alone. His is the kingdom of the heavens and earth. And to Him you will all return."

44/38)
We were not playing a pointless game when We created the heavens and earth and everything in between.

44/39)
We created them in harmony with the truth, but most people do not comprehend.

49/10)
The believers are brothers. So make peace between your brothers. And be mindful of God, so that you may be given mercy.

49/12)
You who believe! Avoid mistrust wherever possible; as some mistrust is sinful. And do not spy on one another or speak ill of people behind their backs. Would any of you like to eat the flesh of your dead brother? No, you would hate it. So be mindful of Allah. Allah is ever relenting, most merciful.

49/13)
Oh you people! We created you all from a single man and a single woman, and made you into races and tribes so that you should get to know one another. In Allah's eyes, the most honored of you are the ones most mindful among you. Allah is all knowing, all aware.

50/16)
We created man – We know what his soul whispers to him. And We are closer to him than (his) jugular vein.

50/17)
When two recorders* set to record, one sitting to the right and one to the left,
* Angels
50/18)
He does not utter a single word without an ever-present watcher.

50/19)
The trance of death will bring the Truth with it: "This is what you tried to escape!"

51/47)
We built the sky with (Our) power and made it vast, We spread out it out (constantly)!*
*Today, it is not disputed that the universe is constantly expanding.

54/32)
We have made it easy to learn lessons from the Quran. Will anyone take heed?

54/52)
And everything they do is noted in their records.
54/53)
And every action, great or small, is recorded.
54/54)
The righteous will live securely among gardens and brooks,
54/55)
At the seat of truthfulness, by an all-powerful Sovereign.

57/1)
What is in the heavens and on earth glorifies Allah. For He is the Almighty, All-Wise.

57/2)
His is the kingdom of the heavens and earth. He gives life and death. And He has power over everything.
57/3)
He is the First and the Last, the Outer and the Inner. And He is knowing of all things.

57/4)
It is He who created the heavens and earth in six days and then established himself on the throne. He knows what enters the earth and what comes out of it; what descends from the sky and what ascends to it. He is with you wherever you are. Allah sees all that you do.

57/5)
His is the kingdom of the heavens and earth. And everything is brought back to Allah.

57/6)
He makes night merge into day and day into night. And He knows fully what is in every heart.

57/9)
It is He who has sent down clear revelations to His Servant to bring you from the depths of darkness into light. And Allah is truly kind and merciful to you.

57/11)
Who will make Allah a good loan? He will more than double it for him and reward him generously.*
* Loan means donated offering

58/7)
Do you not see that Allah knows everything in the heavens and on earth? There is no secret conversation between three people where He is not the fourth, nor between five where He is not the sixth, nor between less or more than that without Him being with them, wherever they may be. On the Day of Resurrection, He will show them what they have done. Allah is truly knowing of all things.

64/14)
... But if you overlook their offences, forgive them, pardon them, then Allah is all forgiving, all merciful.

89/27)
You, soul at peace,
89/28)
Return to your Lord well pleased and well pleasing,
89/29)
Go in among My servants,
89/30)
And into My Paradise!

91/1)
By the sun in its morning brightness!
91/2)
By the moon as it follows it!
91/3)
By the day as it reveals it!*
* the Earth
91/4)
By the night as it covers it!
91/5)
By heaven and He who built it!
91/6)
By the earth and He who spread it!
91/7)
By the soul and He who formed it
91/8)
And inspired it to its own rebellion and piety:
91/9)
The one who purifies his soul lives well,
91/10)
And the one who corrupts it fails.

92/1)

By the covering of night!

92/2)

By the revealing of day!

92/3)

By the male and female He created!

92/4)

Your effort differs greatly.

92/5)

There is the one who gives, who is mindful (of Allah)

92/6)

Who testifies to the best*

* What "the best" (Arab.: "al-husna") is in verse 6 and 9 – the truth par excellence, paradise, the right faith – is open to any interpretation.

92/7)

We shall smooth his way towards ease.

92/8)

There is the one who is miserly and believes to be dependent on no one

92/9)

And declares the best to be a lie,

92/10)

We shall smooth his way towards hardship.

92/11)

And his wealth will not help him as he falls.

92/12)

Our part is to provide guidance.

92/13)

And Ours is the future (in the Hereafter) and the present (in this world).

92/14)

So I warn you about the raging Fire!

92/15)

In which none but the most wicked one will burn,

92/16)

Who denies and turns away.

92/17)

The most pious one will be spared this,

92/18)

Who gives his wealth away as self-purification,

92/19)

Not to return a favor to anyone,

92/20)

But only seeking the face of his Lord,** the Most High,

** To see the "face" (Arab.: "wajh") of his Lord is the insatiable desire of every believer, insatiable possibly also in the Hereafter.

92/21)

And he will certainly be pleased.

94/1)

Did We not relieve your heart for you (Muhammad),

94/2)

And remove the burden from you

94/3)

That weighed so heavily on your back?

94/4)

And (have we not) raised your reputation high?

94/5)

So truly where there is (any) hardship, there is (also) ease!

94/6)

So truly where there is (any) hardship, there is (also) ease!

94/7)

So when you are done (with something), work on

94/8)

And dedicate yourself to your Lord.

95/1)
By the fig and the olive!
95/2)
By Mount Sinai!
95/3)
By this safe city!
95/4)
We created man in the finest state.
95/5)
Then diminished him to the lowest of the low,
95/6)
But those who believe and do good deeds: They will have an unfailing reward.
95/7)
After this, what makes you deny the (Last) Judgement?
95/8)
Is Allah not the most decisive of all judges?

112/1)
Say: "He is God the One,
112/2)
Allah the Absolute.*
* Arab.: "as-samad": The Impenetrable; on whom everything depends and who himself is completely independent; the first cause
112/3)
He begot no one nor was He begotten,
112/4)
And no one is comparable to Him."

2. Spiritual Wisdom of Muhammad (s.a.v.)

The Prophet Muhammad (s.a.v.)

- came into the world in Mecca in 571 and passed away in Medina in 632;
- is considered a messenger of God and a prophet in Islam;
- received the revelation of Allah in the form of the Quran;
- received the first revelation of the Quran in 610 AD at the age of 40.

The hadiths (stories of Muhammad (s.a.v.)) have an important exemplary character for Muslims, since the Prophet was a perfect man in the eyes of Muslims.

Hadiths (Stories) of Muhammad

Bismillahirrahmanirrahiym
In the name of Allah, the Lord of Mercy, the Giver of Mercy!

6/9)
"Wish for greatness before Allah."
It was said: "O Prophet of Allah, what is this?"
He replied: "To the person who meets you ignorant, you meet with mildness and pass by, and to the one who deprives you of something, you bring a benefit."
(told by Ibn Umer r. a.)

11/9)
Do you love it when your heart softens and your prayer becomes visible? Have pity on the orphan, stroke his head and give him some of your food. Through this, your heart softens and you reach your prayer.
(told by Abu Darda r. a.)

12/3)
Make friends among the poor. For on the day of reckoning, the kingdom belongs to them.
(told by Hasan ibn Ali r. a.)

12/8)
Do you know what most ensures people's entry into paradise? Godliness and a beautiful character. Do you know what the greatest reason is for people going to hell? These are two intermediate chambers: the chambers of the mouth and leg.
(told by Abu Hurayrah r. a.)

15/9)
When the believer is measured, a beautiful character is assigned the greatest weight. Surely Allah is indignant at those who do evil, speak evil, and talk insolently.
(told by Abu Darda r. a.)

16/13)
Of deeds, Allah is most fond of feeding a poor person, or paying his debts, or alleviating them of suffering, as good work of a person.
(told by Hakem ibni Umeyr r. a.)

17/8)
Those most pleasing to Allah among you are those who are most beautiful in character. These are such humble people that they are compatible with others and others are compatible with them. Those of you who seem most disliked by Allah are those who pass on what has been said, examine the errors therein, and sow discord between friends.
(told by Enes r. a.)

17/10)
What you love for your self, love for people as well.
(told by the grandfather of Esedül Karsi)

17/16)
Love the good and its qualities. I swear by Allah, blessings and health are with them.
(told by Ebu Said r. a.)

24/3)
Until a person comes to visit his sick friend and sits down, it is as if he has walked on paths of paradise. When he sits down, grace fills him. If he made this visit in the morning, 70,000 angels will pray for him until the evening. If he made this visit in the evening, 70,000 angels will pray for him until the morning.
(told by Ali r. a.)

25/3)
When Allah loves a servant, He closes worldly endeavor to him and opens endeavor for the Hereafter.
(told by Enes r. a.)

25/9)
If one of you loves his neighbor, share the love with him. For this is more constant in togetherness and lasting in friendship.
(told by Mucahid r. a.)

27/1)
When Allah wishes a servant well, He opens the lock of his heart. And He gives him faith and sincerity. And He makes a protection around what reaches his heart and He makes his heart benign, his speech faithful, his morals firm, his ear hearing and his eye seeing.
(transmitted by Ebu Zer r. a.)

29/1)
If you want to do a thing, consider its end well. If the result is goodness, do it; if the result is badness, do without it.
(told by Abdullah ibni Misver r. a.)

37/4)
When the servants are brought to stand on the day of reckoning, a caller will utter the following: "Let those whose reward is with Allah separate themselves and enter that Paradise." It is spoken: "Who is the one whose reward is with Allah?" The caller then says: "Those among men who forgive." As a result, so and so many thousands of people get up and enter paradise without accounting for their actions.
(told by Enes r. a.)

79/8)
On the day of reckoning, the one among you who is closest to me in rank is the one who has the best character among you.
(told by Ali r. a.)

80/5)
When Allah, the Almighty, awards something to a servant, no one can avert it.
(told by Muhallet ibni Ukbe r. a.)

86/8)
When Allah the Almighty wants to execute the decree of destiny, He removes reason from the heads. When the decree is completed, he returns reason. And then repentance comes to them.
(told by Cafer bin Muhammed r. a.)

87/11)
Allah (c. c.), the Almighty, is beautiful and He loves the beautiful. When He has given goods to a servant, He finds pleasure in seeing traces on him. Pride grieves the Creator and angers the creation.
(told by Yahya ibni Cade r. a.)

88/7)
Allah (c. c.) stirred Adam's dough for 40 days and 40 nights. He took it and cut it in half. The good was separated to the right, the bad to the left. Then he stirred the dough again. For this reason, the bad can come out of the good and the good out of the bad.
(told by Ibni Mes´ud r. a.)

92/4)
Allah (c. c.) does not look at your appearance and possessions, but at your hearts and deeds.
(told by Abu Hurayrah r. a.)

96/2)
Being a Muslim is clean, is without dirt. Also be clean and clean yourselves. For the cleanly enter paradise.
(told by Aische r. a.)

99/1)
For someone to be duly Muslim, his tongue must be in harmony with his heart and his heart with his tongue, his deeds and his word must be harmonized, and his neighbor must be safe from his wickedness and sorrow.
(told by Enes r. a.)

101/1)
Truly strong is he who is master of himself in anger.
(told by Hafsa r. a.)

103/4)
Truthfulness leads man to goodness, goodness to paradise. Man speaks and speaks the truth until it is written as "True" in Allah's Kingdom. Lying leads man to manifest sin; manifest sin makes you fall into hell. Man lies and lies until he is written as a "Liar" in Allah's kingdom.
(told by Ibni Mes´ud r. a.)

112/9)
The most beautiful of the beautiful is a beautiful character.
(told by Hasan r. a.)

123/1)
Your Creator is one as well as your Father is one. Your religion and your prophet are also one. The Arab has no superiority over the Persian, and the Persian over the Arab. Once again, the red has no superiority over the dark, and the dark over the red. No nation is superior to another. Only by abstaining from sins can one be superior to the other.
(told by Ebu Said r. a.)

123/3)
When a person entered paradise, he saw that his slave had a higher rank than he did. So he spoke: "Although this one is my slave, should his rank be higher than mine?" Allah replied: "Yes, I have rewarded him as well as you according to your deeds."
(told by Abu Hurayrah r. a.)

127/3)
Man possesses a piece of flesh. If he is healthy, the body is also well. When he suffers, other areas also fare poorly. And that is the heart.
(told by Numan r. a.)

166/6)
Shall I tell you your afflictions and your remedy? Know that your sufferings are your sins. Your remedy, by contrast, is to ask for forgiveness.
(told by Enes r. a.)

192/7)
Faith means knowing with the heart, saying with the language and acting with the guiding personality.
(told by Ali r. a.)

192/11)
Faith means loving Allah.
(told by Abu Hurayrah r. a.)

193/8)
Faith are two equal parts. Half is patience, the other half is gratitude.
(told by Enes r. a.)

194/11)
Good deeds do not perish, sins are not forgotten, and Allah does not die. Do what you want, you will receive the equivalent.
(told by Abu Darda r. a.)

195/1)
The blessing is with your elders. He who does not show mercy to the younger and reverence to the elder is not of us.
(told by Ebu Humame r. a.)

200/16)
Paradise lies beneath the feet of mothers.
(told by Enes r. a.)

204/9)
Shame comes from faith.
(told by Enes r. a.)

205/11)
A beautiful character melts the sins. Just as water melts ice. A bad character corrupts action. Just as vinegar spoils honey.
(told by ibni Abbas r. a.)

207/9)
Prayer consists of worship of God.
Allah shares: "Pray to Me that I may accept your prayer."
(told by Numan ibni Besir r. a.)

234/3)
The sins of the sick person fall like the leaves of the tree.
(told by Halid ibni Abdillah r. a.)

242/2)
The door of repentance is open. Until the sun rises in the evening land,* it will not be closed.
*until the end of the world
(told by Safvan r. a.)

286/12)
The beginning of understanding, according to the belief in Allah, is a sense of shame and a beautiful character.
(told by Enes r. a.)

312/4)
One who promotes knowledge is like one who promotes Allah. To promote knowledge is an essence of Islam. Those who promote this will receive rewards like the prophets.
(told by Enes r. a.)

327/10)
Allah (c. c.) shares: "If My servant intends to do a good deed and does not do it, I write him a good work. If he does it, I write him 10 to 700 good works. If someone intends to do a bad deed, as long as he does nothing, I will not write anything down for him. If he does it, I will write the simple thing down for him."
(told by Abu Hurayrah r. a.)

328/1)
Allah (c. c.) shares: "When My servant comes within a footwidth of Me, I come within a cubit of him. When he comes within a cubit of Me, I come within a fathom of him. When he approaches Me, I approach him continuously."
(told by Enes r. a.)

328/9)
Allah (c. c.) shares: "O Son of Adam! Only when you are a servant to Me, pray to Me, hope for everything from Me and attach nothing to Me, will I forgive what is in you. When you fill the earth and the heavens with your faults and sins and come before Me with them, I meet you with just as much forgiveness and pardon you. To your many sins I then attach no importance."
(told by Abu Darda r. a.)

328/10)
Allah (c. c.) shares: "I am what My servant imagines. (As he imagines Me, so I am) Therefore, let my servant imagine Me as he wishes."
(told by Vasile r. a.)

329/1)
Allah (c. c.) shares: "When a man knows that I am in possession of power, I forgive his sins. As long as he does not associate with Me, I forgive him, I am equanimous."
(told by ibni Abbas r. a.)

331/9)
Gabriel (a. s.) came to me and said: "O Muhammad (s. a. v.), live as long as you want, you will die. Love what you want; ultimately, one day, you will part with it. Do what you want; in the end you will give an account of it."
(told by Cabir r. a.)

331/11)
Moses (a. s.) said: "O my Creator, are You near? Then I speak slowly. Are you far away? So that I should raise my voice. I hear your words but do not see you, where are you?" Allah (c. c.) shared: "I am behind you, in front of you, on your right and also on your left. O Moses (a. s.), when my servant calls me, I am his neighbor, and when he prays, I am with him."
(told by Sevban r. a.)

341/3)
Every good work is an offering.
(told by Bilal r. a.)

343/5)
One wise word heard by someone is better than a year of worship, better than acquiring one hour of knowledge, and better than setting a slave free.
(told by Abu Hurayrah r. a.)

344/4)
The maturity of faith is a beautiful character.
(told by Abu Hurayrah r. a.)

351/2)
The one who eats and is grateful receives the same reward as one who fasts and is patient.
(told by Abu Hurayrah r. a.)

354/3)
Abstaining does not protect you from fate. However, prayer protects. Against what has happened and against what has not happened yet. Thus, O servant of Allah, embrace prayer.
(told by Muaz r. a.)

362/9)
Reading the Quran does not make up the Quran. Reproducing knowledge does not make up knowledge. The Quran is completed with the right faith, knowledge with understanding.
(told by Enes r. a.)

362/12)
Richness does not lie in the possession of many goods. For richness lies in the richness of the soul.
(told by Enes r. a.)

366/6)
Neither for a good nor for a bad person should one wish for death. When he is good, he increases his good. When he is bad, he repents and saves himself.
(told by Abu Hurayrah r. a.)

370/2)
If my love reaches the heart of a servant, Allah forbids his body from going to hell.
(told by Ibn Umer r. a.)

376/4)
On earth, there is no living I over whom a hundred years pass.
(told by Cabir r. a.)

378/12)
There is no one who does not repent when he dies. If he was good, he will regret not doing more good; if he was bad, he will regret why he persisted in the bad.
(told by Abu Hurayrah r. a.)

413/4)
Whoever learns only two hadiths that are useful to him, teaches them to others and uses them, it is better for him than 60 years of worship.
(told by Bera' r. a.)

420/10)
If someone invokes Allah, and if out of fear of Allah tears come out of his eyes and fall to the ground, Allah does not punish that servant on the day of reckoning.
(told by Enes r. a.)

421/3)
When someone sees Me in a dream, he does not go to hell.
(told by Saad ibni Nasire r. a.)

423/9)
If anyone pleases a Muslim after Me, he pleases Me in the grave. And whoever pleases Me in the grave, Allah pleases him on the day of reckoning.
(told by Ibni Mes´ud r. a.)

451/5)
A man who did nothing good all his life removed a thorn from the path. He went so far as to remove the thorns from the tree and put them aside on the ground. This was accepted before Allah and he went to paradise.
(told by Abu Hurayrah r. a.)

2. Hadiths (Stories) of Muhammad

Bismillahirrahmanirrahiym
In the name of Allah, the Lord of Mercy, the Giver of Mercy!

59/48)
Of the religious devotions, Allah (c. c.) is most fond of those which, though few, are performed regularly.
(told by Aise r. a.)

60/49)
Of the religious devotions, Allah (c. c.) is most fond of protecting the tongue.
(told by Ebu Cuheyfe r. a.)

62/54)
Among you, Allah (c. c.) likes best those who eat little and whose bodies are light.
(told by Enes r. a.)

72/71)
Allah (c. c.) has admitted the one who is sinful in faith and an ignorant in life to Paradise because of his generosity.
(told by Enes r. a.)

77/78)
Praise Allah (c. c.), for this praise is a help to both you and your desire.
(told by Ibn Asakir r. a.)

78/79)
Speak about the good sides of your deceased, do not speak about their sins.
(told by Ibn Ömer r. a.)

92/107)

The strongest among you are those who are masters in the moment of anger.

Your kindest, by contrast, are those who forgive even though their power is sufficient.

(told by Ali r. a.)

96/114)

Do your worldly works properly. And do deeds for the Hereafter as if you would die tomorrow.

(told by Enes r. a.)

97/118)

And even if it is from China, accept the knowledge. After all, courting knowledge is a duty of every Muslim.

(told by Enes r. a.)

138/196)

Just as Allah (c. c.) created the disease, He created its remedy. Let yourself be treated in this way.

(told by Enes r. a.)

162/242)

The servant gives a piece of bread as a donation and it grows in the sight of Allah (c. c.) like Mount Uhud.

(told by Ebu Berze r. a.)

228/363)

Spare yourselves from lies; after all, lies cannot be reconciled with faith.

(told by Ebu Bekir r. a.)

244/399)

The eyes of the prophets may sleep, but their hearts do not.

(told by Enes r. a.)

247/406)

The blessing is with your elders.

(told by Ibn Abbas r. a.)

3. Spiritual wisdom of Rumi

Mevlana Dschaladdin Rumi

- was born in 1207 in Afghanistan and died in 1273 in Konya, Turkey;
- was a mystic and one of the most important poets of the Middle Ages writing in Persian.

Today, his written works are known, loved and highly appreciated all over the world.

Spiritual wisdom of Rumi

Mevlana Dschalaladdin Rumi

- The one who learns to kindle light in his heart, to illuminate himself, not even the sun can burn him. If you want to remain luminous like the day, illuminate your self, which resembles the night.

- Observe hundreds of thousands who look alike, and pay attention to the 70 years that differentiate them. Two things can be similar: Both bitter water and sweet water are crystal clear.

- The garden that comes from greenery and flowers is transient, but the rose garden that comes from the mind is always green and beautiful.

- As long as Allah is with you, death as well as life will be beautiful.

- Those who consume honey, do not resent their bee.

- A candle does not lose any of its light when another candle is lit.

- What joy over the one who sees their own mistakes.

- To the fish, everything else is a torment except the sea.

- Both the question and the answer give birth to knowledge.

- I am like a door key calling from the lock. Do you think my words are just words?

- As long as you remain in yourself and worship yourself, no path will be freely opened from you to your I. Do not think that you will find bliss if your existence and self-aggrandizement remain with you. For you still worship the idol of your self.

- The way of our prophet is the way of love.
  We are born of love, our mother is love.

- I am neither Christian nor Jew nor Muslim.
  I am neither from the East nor from the West.
  I have set aside the duality,
  I have seen that both worlds are one.

- Come to yourself, say a brand-new word so that the world will be renewed. Your word must be such a word that it breaks the boundaries of the world. What are boundaries, what are guidelines? You should not know!

- The burning of the wound that comes from the bite of a flea disappears when a snake bites you.

- Love resembles a process, and enduring suffering resembles witnessing. If you don't have witnesses, how are you going to win the case?

- If it were not for the burning of hearts and tears of lovers, there would be no water and no fire on earth.

- If you have no mind, things are bad, but if you have no heart, you are non-existent.

- A person of the mind does not say everything he thinks, but he considers everything he says.

- Do not envy others, for there are many who envy your life.

- Knowledge is a sea without borders. The one who acquires knowledge, by contrast, is a diver who dives into the sea.

- Don't be a drop, bring yourself to the state of a sea. Just as you love the sea, let go of being a drop.

- If the clouds did not cry, how would the green be able to laugh?

- I am known in part by my Self, and in part by my Creator. For one, I need only myself, and for the other, I need the one who understands.

- Be as still as a book beside a simple-minded man.

- The simple-minded ones have little compassion and kindness.

- To be patient about the ignorant makes the knowledgeable shine.

- What is given to a poor person reaches Allah before the poor person holds it in his hands.

- Serenity is born through patience.

- The fact that the rose endures the thorns makes it fragrant.

- Each person is a world. Thoughts make up the human being; what remains are flesh and nerves.

- Everything has been predetermined with destiny. Be content with your destiny so that you can be satisfied.

- Always tell the truth. But not every truth at all times.

- You can't find anything without looking for it. But this friend (Allah) is different; this one you cannot seek until you find Him.

- If you don't have a little light in you, the teachings of outsiders are of no use.

- Place both tips of your fingers on your eyes. Can you still see something of the world? Just because you don't see it doesn't mean that this world doesn't exist.

- Instead of people complaining that there are thorns among roses, they should be grateful that roses were created among thorns.

- Those who strive will obtain the treasure.

- Jewels can be bought with time, but time cannot be bought with jewels.

- What kind of people did I see? They had no clothes on their bodies. What kind of clothes did I see? There were no people in them.

- Whoever you are, still come.

- Patience is the key to joy.

- Know this very well; when your heart becomes the tomb of your secrets, your goals are fulfilled very quickly.

- My silence comes from my nobility. I have an answer to every statement. But; on the one hand, I look to see if the word is a word; on the other, I look to see if the person speaking is a man of stature.

- On this earth, we do not sow any seed other than love.

- Even if his color is dark, if a person has the same intentions with you, call him white: He has your color.

- Even if there is a chain around the neck of a lion, a lion remains a lord for all chain makers.

- Patience is a guide that leads people to their goal the fastest.

- Your heart will take you to the Beloved one day. Your soul will carry you to the Beloved one day. Don't get lost in your pain. Know that the pain you endure will one day be your remedy.

- The heart that knows true love regards even a drop of water with respect.

- An ignorant man does not see the beauty of the rose; he goes and is bothered by the thorns.

- If it is your destiny, you can even receive a lesson from an ant. If it is not your destiny, it would be repugnant to you even if the entire world stretched out before you.

- When you have turned to ashes, wait until you turn into a rose again. And remember not how many times you have become ashes in the past, but how many times you have risen up among the ashes and become a rose again.

- They said: He who is far from the eye, is also far from the heart. I have said: He who found entrance into the heart, what does it matter if He is far from the eye?

- A lover between a hundred people becomes clear like the moon shining in the sky between stars.

- I'm in turmoil, he said. No, he was being tested. If he had realized that, it would have been his salvation.

- If you have a prayer and a request to be everywhere, enter into the hearts; for lovers carry their beloved in their hearts.

- Instead of looking for reasons to be angry or upset with someone, look for ways to love and be loved.

- I have blinded my eyes to the faults of people. You too, like me, look at them with a kind gaze.

- Each of us is an angel with a wing, and we cannot fly until we embrace each other.

- Look! In the case of social crises, quarrels and struggles, the only and strongest reason for their emergence is the absence of love. And the best treatment of this is to seek, live and apply love. When you are tolerant and forgiving, you love. Then you will be loved. If you decide and make an effort along this path, you will achieve everything.

- Not the same language, but whoever shares the same feelings can understand each other.

- In compassion, be like the sun; in generosity, be like flowing water; in humility, be like the earth; in covering faults and shortcomings, be like the night.

- Sometimes angels envy our condition and sometimes even the devil feels disgust at our condition.

- Show mercy to those who are on earth, so that those who are in heavens may show mercy to you. Have compassion with those who are below you so that those who are above you will show you compassion.

- Can there be victory without struggle and patience?

- Before you train your tongue, first train your heart; for the word springs from the heart and comes forth from the tongue.

- No matter how much you know, your words are as much as those around you are capable of understanding.

- The heart is a sea; the tongue is a shore. That which exists in the sea surfaces on the shore.

- The heart is like a garden. Many a thing is sure to grow there. Then sow beautiful things so that beautiful things grow.

- People can achieve anything they strive for. O happy one! Let go of dry prayer. If you want a tree, you must sow seeds.

- Look at the world as not everyone does.

- Do you know what a skill is? That the eyes that look at stones see flowers.

- Your love found no place anywhere. It had a place only in my heart. Now it doesn't fit in my heart either. It streams out of my eyes.

- Love is a disease that has no price and no return. Love does not command, it educates.

- Understanding is knowledge; knowledge is forgiveness.

- When a wave of sorrow hits a person's heart, either he has missed his master or his master has missed him.

- They asked Rumi, "You write so much, you read so much, what do you know?" Rumi replied, "I know my limitations."

- I am not mad with love, friend. But if you were to call, I would come to the deserts. I would not come to You as a lie, but gather my being and come in a simple way. If I knocked on Your door and You said, "Who is it?"; I would not be myself at Your door, but would become You and come. The main thing you said was that I should come, I would not be a burden to the way, would become the way and come.

- Whenever misfortune and calamity reach you, receive them with laughter. You learn gratitude and patience, do not be afraid, the abode of consent is near you.

- Patience is like a bitter herb that quenches pain. It burns and at the same time it treats.

- If everyone has the same opinion, it means that no one is thinking hard enough.

- Our eyes are two, our ears are two, but our mouth is one. You should see a lot, hear a lot, talk little.

- Beautiful times do not come to you. You go to them.

- Words are said according to the one who listens; the tailor sews the clothing according to the size.

- Of this love you suffer no loss, my heart! Even if life fades away, do not be afraid, death is another life.

- Patience is the key to joy.

- My mind asked my heart: "What is faith?" My heart, however, bent to the ear of my mind and said: "Faith is decency."

- Be afraid of aging if you have not understood the value of your youth. Be afraid of being forgotten if you have not left a good work. Be afraid of death if you could not bring yourself to die before death.

- Every raindrop is there to create green. You should not believe that we would have broken down; you should not believe we would have fallen. For another spring, merely our leaves have fallen.

- If one day you have a great sorrow; do not then turn to your Lord and say: "I have a great sorrow." Turn to your suffering and say: "I have a great Lord."

- He who looks with worldly eyes sees the face; he who looks with the eyes of the heart sees the essence of man.

- What you are looking for is you. If you look for bad, you are a bad person; if you look for love, you are a lover.

- Don't worry about it, my heart. Even if no one knows and no one understands that you are tired. The Lord knows about your truthfulness.

- An Iranian poet says: "If you fly to love, your wings will burn." Thereupon Rumi says: "If you don't fly to love, what do you have wings for?"

- When it all comes crashing down on you and brings you to a point where you can't take it anymore, definitely don't give up! For there is the place where your destiny turns.

- The less high you fly, the less you hurt yourself when you fall. Leave pride, be humble!

- Your thoughts reflect your words; your words reflect your actions; and your actions reflect your destiny. Think beautiful, live beautiful!

- Stop being marble in castles. Be earth so that roses grow on your chest.

- It is not easy to be a candle. To give off light, one must first burn.

- Suffering always shows man a way.

- Death comes last of all, yet we say it is too soon.

- If suffering causes you to invoke Allah in secret, it is more valuable than all the goods on earth.

- This life of yours, in which you find yourself, of the single moment, you should know as an opportunity. And be involved in it. Neither grieve over your past, nor fear the future!

- To converse with one who is ignorant is burdensome for one who knows. Because the ignorant person says everything that comes to his mind.

- Whoever is patient, to him comes the daily bread. To work and toil with excessive ambition is impatience.

- Suppose you have conquered the entire east and west, you have gained dominion over every place. Since this rule will not stay, assume it is lightning; it strikes and disappears. O you free sleeper, consider a possession that does not last forever as a dream.

- A person who considers himself incomplete rides ten horses to maturity. By contrast, a person who thinks he is mature does not reach Allah because of this conceit of his.

- Since you cannot close the sins and mistakes of others, close your own eyes!

- You, my heart's left side. I put you to my mind; my mind could not take you in. I left You to my heart, it did not get tired of You!

- To the question: "What is the value of a human being?" Rumi answered briefly, but very profoundly: "His value is what he's looking for."

- Life is a sleep; man awakens when he dies. Act early and wake up before you die.

- Love is such a vast, infinite sea that it has neither a beginning nor an end.

- Heart! Let them call you mad, call you insane, call you mortally in love, call you defeated, call you living in ignominy of defeat. But O heart, let them not call you drunkard of victory. To you they shall not say, "He could not break your heart." O heart, value your defeat as holy. Break your heart and become heart. Collect scents from paradise. And also from even greater distances.

- The one with decency keeps silent out of decency. And the one without decency thinks he has silenced him.

- Hopelessness is the most beautiful sign that comes from Allah. It indicates that it is time to pray. When tears come out of your eyes and sadness is on your beautiful face, it means your Lord has missed you, he has wanted to hear your voice.

- The sublimity of a goal becomes clear through the hardships of the way.

- Suppose you have conquered all the West, all the East; is it not the case that these will not remain, that you will go away and perish?

- Pour the water of your life force into the sea; become a boundless, endless sea.

- He who sees a beautiful dream while awake is a knower.

- There are many people whose eyes see, but the heart sleeps.

- Be food, be strength, immerse yourself in thought; you were milk, now become a lion in forests.

- May he walk slowly, may he run swiftly, he who seeks will find. Embrace the wish with both hands; for it is the wish that is a guide to the right path.

- Look for the source within yourself.

- The words of water, the words of earth, the words of clay are heard and understood by the heart society.

- Whatever you desire, seek it within yourself!
  There is a life force in your life force, seek it!
  There is a treasure in your mountain, search for it!
  If you are looking for the wandering dervish;
  Don't look for him outside of yourself,
  Look for him in yourself!

- I do not sell freedom for servitude.

- Do not go to the village of hopelessness; there are hopes.
  Don't go toward the darkness; there are suns.

- Understanding is knowledge; knowledge is forgiveness.

- As you look, so you see.

- For us, practice patience for a few more days;
  because patience is the key to joy.

- A book is the food of the soul and medicine for the mind.

- Who said that the rose lives under the protection of the thorn?
  The reputation of the thorn owes only to the rose!

- There are so many scholars who have no part in true knowledge, true education. Such a scholar is a reciter of knowledge; he is not a lover of knowledge.

- If you knock on the door of meanings, it will be opened for you.

- Man is so great, so sublime, that it cannot be grasped with thought.

- You are like the green on the earth, your feet are bound ...

- Man is a jewel, while heaven is a sign for man; everything proceeds in stages, but the purpose is man.

- The shadow of Allah (c. c.) is over the head of the servant; he who seeks will ultimately find.

- Whoever belongs to Allah (c. c.), Allah (c. c.) also belongs to him.

- The one who opens the door to his heart sees a sun (atom) in every smallest part.

- The division and dispute between religions is due to the way of progress, not the truthfulness of the path.

- In truth, the one whom everyone worships is only Allah (c. c.). But the ways are different; everyone's taste varies.

- My faith is to live in love ...

- Allah (c. c.) created everyone for a specific task. In everyone's chest He has put the desire to be busy with an activity.

4. Spiritual Wisdom of the Four Great Caliphs

4.1 Caliph Ebu Bekir

The lineage of Caliph Ebu Bekir (r. a.) was of kinship with Prophet Muhammad (s. a. v.) through their grandparents. He is also descended from the nomadic Kureysh tribe.

Caliph Ebu Bekir (r. a.) came into the world about two years later than Prophet Muhammad (s. a. v.), that is, around the year 573 AD.

Like the other great caliphs, he was a faithful companion and lover of Prophet Muhammad (s. a. v.).

He was sincere, truthful and virtuous. He died at the age of 63, in 636 AD.

Spiritual Wisdom of Caliph Ebu Bekir (r. a.)

- The closest to Allah (c. c.) among people is the one who loves Him the most.

- Your love should not be excessive; your not loving should not be exhausting.

- Many words make a person forgetful.

- Think carefully about what you say, when you say it, and to whom you say it.

- If you miss a good deed, try to make it up. When you achieve it, look to get ahead of it. Strive to make even more beautiful things.

- Doing good to people protects the person from misfortune and calamity.

- Don't prepare a grave for yourself, but prepare yourself for the grave.

- To renounce the bad is better than to ask for the good.

- Those who are attached to Prophet Muhammad (s. a. v.) should know, he died. Whoever is connected to Allah (c. c.) should know that Allah (c. c.) does not die.
  (The words of Caliph Ebu Bekir (r. a.) to the Muslims when Muhammad (s. a. v.) passed away, which appeased them).

- The secret to speaking concisely is to abandon unnecessary words.

- Be patient, the beginning of all things is patience.

- Move four things to four places: sleep to the grave; comfort to the passage into the other world; pride to the scales of deeds; and desire to paradise.

- A mature person accepts forgiveness as his debt and doing good as his duty.

- Allah (c. c.) does not agree with the inactive word of the servant.

- Many words make a person forgetful.

- Books are the gardens of wise people.

- Even if you show repentance 70 times, still repent again.

- Just as Allah (c. c.) sees what is external to you, He also sees what is within you.

- Among people, the closest to Allah (c. c.) is the one who loves Him the most.

- Consider your urges as deceased and serve Allah (c. c.) as if you were seeing Him.

4.2 Caliph Umer

Caliph Umer (r. a.) came from the nomadic tribe of Kureysh. He came into the world 40 years before the Hejira (622 AD, the resettlement of Muslims and Prophet Muhammad from Mecca to Medina: Beginning of the Muslim calendar), thus 582 AD.

Like the other great caliphs, he was a faithful companion and lover of Prophet Muhammad (s. a. v.).

For Allah (c. c.) and the Prophet (s. a. v.), he lived with utmost effort. During the first years of the founding of the religion, he provided great support for Prophet Muhammad (s. a. v.) because of his courage and strength.

Caliph Umer (r. a.) died in 645 AD at the age of 63.

Spiritual Wisdom of Caliph Umer

- For Allah, there is no behavior that He prefers than conquering anger.

- From the question a person asks, I determine the level of his intelligence.

- Those who do not know the bad, fall into its trap.

- Show little affection to the worldly so that you live freely.

- Be strong without using force, be mild without showing weakness.

- Don't be deceived by a person's fame and appearance, don't look at his prayer and observance of duties, look at his intellect and sincerity.

- Before you question things that didn't happen, try to learn a lesson from the things that did happen.

- The honor of mankind is carried out with its intellect, nobility with its faith, its individuality with its morals and ethics.

- In order to be able to move people for the better, we must first move ourselves for the better.

- The one who gives up laughing a lot is given dignity.

- Not knowing what was better for me, I did not pay attention to deprivation or prosperity in any way.

4.3 Caliph Osman

Caliph Osman (r. a.) came from the nomadic tribe of Kureysh. He came into the world 47 years before the Hejira (622 AD), thus in 575 AD.

Like the other great caliphs, he was a faithful companion and lover of Prophet Muhammad (s. a. v.).

Caliph Osman (r. a.) is a model of decency and nobility for Muslims. He gave away large portions of his wealth for Islam.

Caliph Osman (r. a.) died in 657 AD at the age of 82.

Spiritual Wisdom of Caliph Osman

- The heart darkens with concern for the world; with concern for eternity, it becomes wise.

- Before death reaches you, immediately do the good you can do.

- Stay away from alcohol, because alcohol is the key to everything bad.

- Learn a lesson from the past and work to do good.

- Apart from Allah, there is no true refuge.

- Take truly, give truly.

- Allah (c. c.) does not make a wish from something that He does not bestow.

- When you face difficulties, practice patience. Because there are no difficulties, after which no relief appears.

4.4 Caliph Ali

Caliph Ali (r. a.) came from the Tribe of Kureysh. He is the son of Ebu Talib, the uncle of Prophet Muhammad (s. a. v).

Caliph Ali (r. a.) came into the world 8 to 10 years before the Hejira (622 A.D.).

Like the other great caliphs, he was a faithful companion and lover of Prophet Muhammad (s. a. v.).

He was brave, strong and virtuous.

Caliph Ali (r. a.) died at the age of 63.

Spiritual Wisdom of Caliph Ali

- To make sure your kids are in charge later, give them good books today.

- Do not be attached to anything in the world, only in this way can you preserve your freedom.

- To achieve one's goal, patience is the key; the result of effort is victory. Every wish that wants to be realized has its time; fate sets this moment in motion and gives it an exterior.

- If the heart is blind, there is no use for the eyes to see.

- Treat people so well that even your enemy cries over your death.

- Today is the day of action, there is no reckoning. Tomorrow, however, there will be a reckoning, there will be no possibility of action then.

- Avoiding sins is the foundation of faith.

- The one who rises with knowledge does not die.

- The one who laughs a lot loses dignity.

- He who has little intellect cannot hold his tongue.

- Don't look at the one who is speaking, look at what is being said.

- The word is like medicine; little of it gives life, too much of it causes death.

- A scholar lives even when he dies; by contrast, an ignorant person dies during his life.

- I wanted to be highly placed. I found that in humility.

- If you are in the right, you shall not surrender to anyone.

- At no time did I win a discussion against an ignorant person.

- Don't be too hard or you'll break. Don't be too soft, or you will be oppressed.

- If you open your secrets to this or that, be okay with the disgrace that will come to you.

- Prayer is the believer's weapon and the pillar of faith. It is holy light in heaven and on earth.

- The feet of the brave were created for endurance, and the feet of the cowardly were created for flight.

- Knowledge is superior to possession. For you protect your possessions, but your knowledge protects you.

- In this chest of mine there is much knowledge hidden. O if only I could find gentlemen capable of carrying it!

- You humans believe that you are meaningless. In truth, there is a vast universe hidden within you.

Explanations of the abbreviations in this book

(c. c.) Celle celaluhu: Is expressed to exalt Allah.
Used only in the context of Allah.

(s. a. v.) Sallallahu aleyhi ve sellem: May blessings and greetings be upon Muhammad.
Used only in connection with Muhammad.

(a. s.) Aleyhisselam: May Allah's greetings be with him.
Used only in connection with prophets.

(r. a.) Radiyallahu anh: May Allah be pleased with him/her.
Used only in the context of companions during Muhammad's lifetime and some great Islamic figures.

Bibliography

Title: The Quran – The Holy Book of Islam
Translation from Arabic into German: Max Henning
German revision: Murad Wilfried Hofmann.
English translation from German into English: Henry Whittlesey (upon consultation of
translation from Arabic by M.A.S. Abdel Haleem)
Publisher: Cağrı Yayınları

Title: Ramuz el-Ehadis
Hadisler Deryası
Author: Ahmed Ziyaüddin Gümüşhanevi, Abdülaziz Bekkine
Printing house: Milsan Basın Sanayii A. Ş.

Title: Sahih-i Buhari ver Tercemesi
Author: Mehmed Sofuoglu
Publisher: Ötüken

Title: Mevlana Dergahından Sözler
Author: Dr. Yaşar Ateşoğlu
Publisher: Neden Kitap Yayımcılık

Title: Mevlana´dan düşündüren Sözler
Author: Baki Apaydın
Publisher: Tutku Yayınevi

Title: Mevlana´dan düşündüren Sözler
Author: Şaban Karaköse
Publisher: Yediveren Yayınları

All quotes and wisdom were individually selected from Turkish media by the author and translated initially into German by the author and then from German into English by Henry Whittlesey.